Raising Them Right –

One Moment at a Time

By Arushi Mahajan

Dedication

With the grace of Guru Ji,

To every parent who wakes up every day with love in their heart and worry on their mind, trying their best. To my own mother, who taught me resilience, and to my children—who teach me something new every single day. To every teacher, caregiver, and educator walking hand in hand with today's parents—this book is for you.

Acknowledgment

No journey is ever walked alone —
and this book is no exception.

I express my heartfelt gratitude to
my family, especially my mother,
who showed me what resilience
truly means. To my supportive
husband — your strength through
storms has kept me grounded and
growing. To my children, who have
been my greatest teachers —
thank you for helping me
rediscover wonder, patience, and
unconditional love. A special thank
you to my mentor Mr. Arun
Sharma, friends, and well-wishers
who have encouraged me to keep
moving forward, even when the
road felt uncertain.

To every parent reading this —
thank you. You are the reason this
book exists. May it remind you of
your strength, your softness, and
your incredible role in shaping the
future.

About the Author

Arushi Mahajan is an educator, Principal at GD Goenka Toddler House, President Awardee in Scouts and Guides, and a certified teacher trainer and a mother . With a background in aviation and education, she blends real-life experience with heartfelt parenting insights.

Table of Contents

Chapter 1:

The Heart of Connection

"Connection is why we're here. It is what gives purpose and meaning to our lives." – Brené Brown

Parenting, at its very core, is about connection. Not control. Not perfection. Not having all the answers. But about being present — emotionally available, tuned in, and committed to understanding the little human who looks up at you with trusting eyes. When we pause long enough to truly see our children — beyond their behavior, their moods, or their messes — we begin to build something far more powerful than obedience. We build trust. We build security. We build love that lasts.

—

A Real-Life Moment: Meera and Aarav

Meera, a working mother of two, often found herself in a hurry. One evening, her 4-year-old son Aarav threw his shoes across the room and refused to eat dinner. "Why are you acting like this again?" she snapped, tired after a long day.

But something in her paused. She sat beside him, looked him in the eye, and said softly, "You didn't have a good day, did you?" Aarav's eyes filled with tears. "You didn't come to pick me today. I waited…"That evening, Meera didn't force dinner or discipline. She held her son and whispered, "I missed you too. "That five-minute pause, that tiny act of connection, changed the energy of their home.

Why Connection Works

Brain science now tells us what our hearts already knew: children thrive in connection. Dr. Dan Siegel, a renowned psychiatrist, explains in his "Whole-Brain Child" approach that secure attachments — where children feel seen, soothed, and safe — build emotional intelligence and long-term well-being. When a child acts out, it's often a cry not for punishment but for reconnection. Connection doesn't spoil children. It stabilizes them.

What Connection Looks Like in Real Life

- Kneeling down to your child's level when they're upset

- Saying "I'm here" instead of "Stop crying!"

- Listening more than instructing

- Making time, even just 10 minutes of full attention daily

- Naming emotions aloud: "You seem really frustrated. Do you want to talk about it or should we just sit together for a bit?"

—

Arushi's Personal Reflection

I remember a moment from my early motherhood days. My daughter was crying nonstop one evening. I had barely slept. My patience had worn thin. But then I reminded myself of the very truth I wanted to teach other parents — children don't need perfect parents. They need present ones. So I simply lay down beside her, pulled her into my arms, and hummed her favorite tune. No scolding. No advice. Just presence. And in that moment, she quieted, not because I controlled her, but because she felt safe.

That's the heart of connection.

Reflection Prompt for You
Think of a moment when your child was acting out.

- What did you do?

- Could connection have helped more than correction?

- How might you respond differently next time?

Take a minute to jot down what made that moment hard — and what could help next time.

Practice Steps: Building the Connection Muscle

Here are some simple yet powerful steps to strengthen your bond:

1. Pause Before You React

Instead of jumping into discipline mode, take a breath. Ask, "What is my child feeling right now?"

2. Validate Feelings

Even if the behavior needs correction, begin with empathy: "I understand you're angry…"

3. Create Rituals of Connection

Morning hugs, bedtime chats, Friday dance parties — make connection a habit.

4. Use Gentle Eye Contact

Your eyes can say, "You matter to me," without a single word.

5.   Repair After Ruptures

Every parent loses their temper. But what matters most is what you do after. Say, "I'm sorry I yelled. I want to do better."

One Moment at a Time

Connection isn't a one-time act. It's built in the quiet, daily interactions. In the way we look at our children when they speak. In the way we hold their hand across a busy road. In how we pause our phones when they call, "Mumma, see this! "As you move through this book, remember: you don't need to be a perfect parent. You just need to be a connected one.

Chapter 2:

Handling Tantrums with Heart

"Behind every tantrum is an unmet need, an overwhelmed mind, and a child looking for help in the only way they know."

If there's one thing that tests even the calmest parent, it's a full-blown tantrum — screaming, kicking, crying in the middle of the grocery store, or storming out of the room. But tantrums aren't just misbehavior. They are messages. Signals that something deeper is going on inside a child's brain and heart.

How we respond in those high-voltage moments defines the kind of emotional safety our child feels.

A Real-Life Story: Nikhil in the Toy Store

Riya had promised her 5-year-old son, Nikhil, that they were going to the supermarket "just for groceries." But the moment they passed the toy aisle, Nikhil saw a racing car he'd seen on TV. "I want that one!" he yelled, grabbing at the shelf. Riya calmly reminded him of their deal. But within seconds, he dropped to the floor, screaming. People stared. Her heart pounded. She wanted to scold him, threaten to leave, or walk away in frustration. But instead, she sat beside him, placed a gentle hand on his back, and whispered, "It's hard, isn't it? You really wanted that car. "He didn't stop immediately. But he heard her. She stayed with him, offering connection instead of control. After five long minutes, he got up, teary-eyed but calmer. They walked out, hand in hand.

The car stayed on the shelf — but the bond grew stronger.

Why Do Tantrums Happen?

Tantrums are a biological response, not moral failings. The emotional center of a child's brain — the amygdala — is still developing. When children feel overwhelmed (hungry, tired, overstimulated, frustrated), their brain floods with emotion, and their "thinking brain" temporarily shuts down. In that moment, logic doesn't work. They're not "bad kids" being "manipulative" — they're tiny humans having a meltdown because their brain literally can't cope. Our job is to be their calm — not their storm.

What Not to Say During a Tantrum

- "Stop it right now!"

- "You're being ridiculous!"

- "If you don't stop, I'll leave you here!"

- "Why are you always like this?"

These responses shame or threaten children, making them feel unsafe — and often prolonging the meltdown.

What to Say Instead
- "I'm right here. You're safe."

- "It's okay to be upset. Let's breathe together."

- "I can see you're having a really hard time."

- "Do you want a hug, or some space?"

Children may not respond right away. But your calm becomes their anchor.

Arushi's Reflection

I still remember the first time my daughter had a public tantrum. I felt eyes burning into my back — people judging, whispering. My instinct was to hush her fast, to control the situation for others' comfort. But deep inside, I knew what I had always believed — my child needs my support more than strangers need silence. So I knelt down, whispered words of reassurance, and let her big feelings be okay. From that day, I promised myself: My child's dignity is more important than anyone's opinion.

Reflection Prompt

- When your child last had a meltdown, how did you respond?

- What triggered it? Was it hunger, tiredness, or emotional overload?

•   What did you need in that moment — and what did your child need?

Practice Steps: Handling Tantrums with Heart

1.   Stay Physically Close, Emotionally Present

Your calm presence regulates their nervous system. Don't abandon or isolate.

2.   Avoid "Fixing" or Explaining in the Moment

When the brain is in meltdown mode, explanations don't help. Save the talk for later.

3.   Offer Safe Touch

A hand on the back, an open hug — if your child is open to it.

4.   Name the Feeling, Hold the Limit

"You're angry you can't have the toy. I won't buy it, but I understand."

5.   Debrief Later

When emotions have settled, reflect gently: "Next time, let's try saying what you want calmly."

Chapter 3:

The Power of Positive Discipline

"Discipline is not about punishment; it's about teaching. Not about control; but guidance."

The word discipline comes from the Latin word disciplina, meaning "instruction" or "teaching." Yet somewhere along the way, it began to be confused with punishment — time-outs, raised voices, consequences meant to "make them learn. "But children don't learn from fear. They learn from connection. They don't grow through punishment. They grow through guidance. Positive discipline is about helping a child understand right from wrong without making them feel wrong in the process.

Real-Life Story: Ishaan and the Broken Vase

Eight-year-old Ishaan was playing football in the hallway, even after being told not to. His kick hit a table, and the decorative glass vase shattered. His mother, Radhika, rushed into the room. His face said it all — fear, guilt, and regret. He braced himself for the yelling. But instead, Radhika paused, took a breath, and said, "Ishaan, I know you love football. But playing here broke something valuable. Let's clean this up together, and then we'll talk. "Later, when things had calmed, she sat with him. "I'm not angry. I just want you to understand why we don't play indoors. What can we do next time?" They came up with a plan: football in the garden only. He didn't just clean up glass. He cleaned up his mistake — with support, not shame.

Why Positive Discipline Works

Children are not born knowing how to control impulses, manage emotions, or weigh consequences. These are learned skills — and they take years to develop.

Positive discipline teaches by:

- Modeling respect and empathy.

- Encouraging accountability without humiliation.

- Teaching problem-solving, not blind obedience.

- Strengthening trust, rather than fear-based compliance.

When discipline is rooted in love,
it raises children who are
internally motivated to do the right
thing — not just to avoid getting
in trouble.

Common Misconceptions

"If I don't punish them, they'll walk
all over me."

Positive discipline doesn't mean
permissiveness. It means being
firm and kind, setting clear
boundaries with warmth.

"They won't take me seriously if I
don't yell."

Children listen better when they
feel safe. Yelling teaches fear,
not respect.

"I turned out fine, and I was
spanked."

Survival is not the same as
thriving. Just because we

endured something doesn't make it the best way.

☐

Arushi's Reflection
I recall a moment with my son when he hit his sister out of frustration. My first instinct was to scold him loudly — but something in me paused. I knelt beside him, looked into his eyes and said, "I know you're upset, but hurting is not okay. You're allowed to be angry, but hands are for helping. "Instead of sending him away, I stayed. We breathed together, hugged, and talked about how to express big feelings. That one moment taught me — discipline without connection is just noise. But discipline with understanding becomes a life lesson.

☐

Reflection Prompt

- When your child misbehaves, what's your first reaction?

- Is it guided by fear, habit, or calm intention?

- What would it look like to teach rather than punish in that moment?

Practice Steps: Discipline That Builds, Not Breaks

1. Pause Before You React

Take a deep breath. Responding calmly prevents escalation.

2. Name the Behavior, Not the Child

"Throwing toys is not okay." instead of "You're so naughty!"

3. Validate Feelings, Set Clear Limits

"I see you're angry. But we don't hit. Let's try saying 'I'm mad!' instead."

4.   Teach a Better Way

Every "don't do this" should be paired with a "do this instead."

5.   Follow Through with Kind Consequences

If rules are broken, consequences should be natural, related, and respectful — not harsh.

☐

Key Takeaway

Positive discipline isn't about ignoring misbehavior. It's about seeing behavior as communication, and choosing to respond with wisdom rather than impulse.

Our children aren't learning to
avoid mistakes — they're learning
how to repair them. And that's
what life is all about.

Time and Real Time –
ig the Balance

Technology is a tool — not a
replacement for presence."

It's the new age babysitter,
entertainer, and occasional savior
during restaurant meltdowns —
screens. From educational videos
to mobile games, screens are
everywhere. And let's admit it —
as parents, sometimes they help
us survive the day. But as screen
time increases, so does
something else: the distance
between parent and child. So
how do we walk the fine line
between digital convenience and
meaningful connection?

Real-Life Story: Kavya and the Silent Dinner

Every evening, Kavya would return home to her 6-year-old daughter, Myra, already glued to her iPad. Dinner was no different — quiet bites, blank stares at cartoon videos. One day, Kavya noticed Myra barely responding to questions. Her words had become fewer. Her laughter, rarer. That night, Kavya made a bold decision — "No screens after 6 PM. "Instead, they baked cookies, spilled flour everywhere, giggled at burnt edges, and laughed more in one evening than they had in a week. Myra's vocabulary returned. So did her hugs.

Why It Works

Children don't just need content — they need connection. Screens can delay language development, reduce attention spans, and replace crucial emotional bonding moments, especially in early years. But when used wisely, technology can support learning — if balanced with rich real-world interactions.

Signs Screen Time is Taking Over

- Less eye contact, more eye strain.

- Shorter attention spans.

- Meltdowns when the device is taken away.

- Reduced creativity in play.

Practical Steps to Find the Balance

1. Set Screen-Free Zones

Bedrooms and dining tables should be screen-free sanctuaries.

2.   Schedule Tech Time

Instead of "whenever," set defined, age-appropriate limits. Eg: 30 mins a day for children under 6.

3.   Replace with Engagement, Not Emptiness

Don't just "remove" screens — replace them. Reading, puzzles, storytelling, chores done together.

4.   Watch Together

If they're watching something, sit with them. Pause, discuss, make it interactive.

5.   Be a Role Model

Kids don't do what we say; they do what we do. Your phone habits matter too.

Reflection Prompt

- What message does my child receive when I'm constantly on my phone?

- How can I shift our evening routine from "passive" to "present"?

Key Takeaway

Screens are not the enemy — disconnection is.

When used wisely, screens can educate. But they should never replace the warmth of your voice, the feel of your touch, or the sparkle of eye contact.

Chapter 5:

**Building Emotional Intelligence
– Name It to Tame It**

"Children are not born with emotional control — they learn it from us."

Tantrums, outbursts, whining, sulking — these aren't just misbehaviors. They're emotional signals. Think of a child as a cup filled with feelings — but no straw. They feel everything, but they don't always know how to express it. That's where we come in. Teaching emotional intelligence isn't a one-time lesson — it's a daily language. And the earlier we start, the stronger their emotional foundation becomes.

☐

Real-Life Story: Arav and the Monster Drawing

4-year-old Arav returned from school cranky and aggressive. He pushed his blocks, yelled at his sister, and then burst into tears. Instead of scolding him, his father sat beside him with paper and crayons. "Let's draw how you feel. "Arav drew a giant red monster with tears. "That's a big feeling," his father said. "Want to talk about it? "Turns out, Arav had been ignored by a friend at school. That drawing turned a tantrum into a conversation.

☐

Why It Works
When children learn to name their emotions, they learn to tame them.

Labeling feelings activates the brain's thinking center, calming the emotional storm.

☐

Steps to Build Emotional Intelligence

1.Model Emotion Words Daily

"I'm feeling tired today, so I'll take a break."

"I was frustrated, but I took deep breaths."

2.Teach Them the Emotional Vocabulary

Go beyond "happy/sad." Teach: excited, jealous, nervous, proud, embarrassed.

3.Validate First, Fix Later

"It's okay to feel angry." Instead of "Stop crying!"

Acknowledgement soothes.

4.Create an Emotion Corner

A cozy place with emotion charts, drawing tools, books — where children can cool down and explore feelings.

5.   Use Stories and Role-Play

Ask: "How do you think the lion felt when he lost his friend?"

It builds empathy and insight.

☐

Arushi's Reflection

There were moments when my own child's tears would trigger my anxiety. But over time, I learned that calming myself was the first step to helping them. I remember sitting in a car, both of us crying — me, out of frustration; my child, out of helplessness. That day, I whispered, "I'm here. We'll get through this together. "And that made all the difference.

☐

Reflection Prompt

• How do I respond to my child's big emotions?

• Do I listen, or do I rush to "fix" it?

☐

Key Takeaway

Children don't need perfect parents.

They need emotionally available ones — who show them how to feel, fall apart, and find calm again. conscious, connected parenting. This approach emphasizes empathy, understanding, and mutual respect to build a strong bond between parent and child.

Chapter 6:

Discipline or Punishment? – Choosing Connection Over Control

"Discipline teaches. Punishment controls. Only one builds character."
It's bedtime. Your child refuses to brush. You snap, "If you don't listen, no cartoon tomorrow! "Sound familiar? We've all been there. And in that moment, it feels like the only way to gain control. But discipline isn't about control. It's about guidance.
Children misbehave not because they want to irritate us, but because they are still learning how to behave. Our response can either teach them better — or just scare them silent.

Real-Life Story: The Broken Vase Incident

7-year-old Diya was playing indoors when a loud crash echoed. Her mother rushed in to find her favorite vase shattered. Diya froze, expecting to be yelled at. Instead, her mother knelt down and said, "I see you're scared. Can we talk about what happened?"
Diya burst into tears, admitted it was her fault, and they cleaned up together.
That moment taught Diya responsibility — not fear.

Why It Works

Fear might bring short-term obedience but long-term resentment. Connection-based discipline fosters self-awareness, accountability, and trust.

Difference Between Discipline and Punishment

- **Punishment** focuses on what *not* to do.
- **Discipline** teaches what *to* do instead.
- **Punishment** is reactive. **Discipline** is proactive.
- **Punishment** isolates. **Discipline** connects.

Practical Steps to Positive Discipline

1. Set Clear Expectations Before, Not After
2. Use Natural Consequences (Not Shame)
3. Repair, Don't Repeat – After outbursts, reconnect strategies. Each reflection is rooted in modern parenting challenges and encourages conscious, connected parenting. This approach emphasizes empathy, understanding, and mutual respect to build a strong bond between parent and child.4.

Stay Calm, Even If They Aren't
5. Offer Choices When Possible

Reflection Prompt

- What did I learn about discipline
as a child?
- Am I repeating a pattern, or
rewriting one?

Key Takeaway
Children remember how we
corrected them far longer than
what we corrected. Choose
compassion. That's the real
discipline.

Chapter 7:

When Comparison Creeps In – Raising *This* Child, Not *That* One

"Comparison is the thief of joy — and connection. "Look at Rhea, she eats on her own!"
"Why can't you be like your cousin who always listens?
"These seemingly harmless comments actually plant the deepest seeds of self-doubt in a child. Every child is unique — yet comparison pushes them into a mold that was never meant for them.

Real-Life Story: Aarav and the Art Class

Aarav, 5, loved painting bold, messy canvases — full of imagination. One day, a relative said, "Why don't you draw neatly like your friend? His work looks like a real painting. "Aarav stopped painting for weeks. His mother noticed. Instead of coaxing him, she sat beside him one afternoon and said, "I miss your wild, happy colors. "That night, he picked up his brush again.

Why It Works

Children bloom in environments where they're celebrated — not compared.
When comparison enters, creativity, confidence, and connection exit.

What Comparison Does

- Diminishes self-worth
- Breeds resentment among siblings/friends
- Damages parent-child trust
- Prevents authentic self-

expression

Steps to Break the Comparison Cycle

1. Notice Your Words – Even subtle ones matter
2. Celebrate Effort Over Outcome
3. Reframe Praise – "I love how *you* tried!"
4. Avoid Sibling Benchmarks
5. Let Them Lead Their Path

Arushi's Reflection

I too faced comparison — in school, in extended family, even as a mother. It took time to realize I wasn't meant to be like anyone else.
Today, I consciously remind my children, "Your race, your pace."

Reflection Prompt

- Do I unintentionally compare my

child — even in thoughts?
- How can I affirm my child's
individuality this week?

Key Takeaway

The best gift you can give your
child is freedom from comparison.
Help them grow into themselves
— not someone else.

Chapter 8:

**Screens and Scenes –
Parenting in the Digital Age**

"Technology is a tool, not a
parent."
The digital world is here to stay
— from lullabies on YouTube to
teens scrolling through social
media. As parents, our challenge
is not to ban screens, but to build
boundaries and balance.

***Real-Life Story: The Case of
the Tablet Tantrum***

Mihir, 6, would throw massive
tantrums every time his screen
time ended. His parents tried
hiding the tablet, yelling, even
bribing — nothing worked. Then
they made a small shift: they
began watching videos with him,
discussing them, and then jointly
decided screen schedules. Over

time, Mihir's outbursts reduced drastically.

Why It Works

When parents engage instead of just enforcing, children feel involved — not controlled. This builds healthy tech habits, instead of rebellion.

Signs Screen Time May Be Harming

- Difficulty sleeping
- Increased irritability
- Lack of interest in physical play
- Avoidance of face-to-face conversation

Smart Steps for Screen Balance

1. Create Screen-Free Zones (like meals and bedrooms)

2. Co-View and Co-Engage
3. Prioritize Offline Activities
4. Set Predictable Routines
(same screen time daily)
5. Teach Critical Thinking (What
did you learn? What did you
feel?)

Reflection Prompt

- How is screen time impacting
our family dynamics?
- Do I model the screen habits I
want my child to have?

Key Takeaway

Screens are here, but so is your
power to lead by example.
Connect before you correct.

Chapter 9:

The Power of "I'm Sorry" – When Parents Make Mistakes

"Strong parents don't pretend to be perfect. They repair."
There's no such thing as a perfect parent — just intentional ones. There will be days when you shout too loudly, miss your child's emotions, or act unfairly. But what you do *after* matters more than what you did.

Real-Life Story: A Morning Gone Wrong

It was a rushed morning. Sia, a working mom, scolded her daughter for forgetting her water bottle. Her daughter quietly left for school, eyes downcast. By noon, guilt crept in. Sia texted, "Mommy is sorry for being harsh.

I love you. "That evening, her daughter hugged her tighter than ever before.

Why It Works

Apologizing models emotional maturity and humility. It teaches children that everyone makes mistakes — and that making amends builds trust. The Myth of Parental Perfection
Children don't need perfect parents. They need *present* parents — ones who show up, own up, and grow up.

Ways to Apologize Authentically
1. Be Specific – "I'm sorry I yelled" instead of "Sorry if I upset you"
2. Avoid Justifying – Don't follow with "...but you made me angry"
3. Invite Dialogue – "How did that make you feel?"

4. Repair with Action – A hug, a talk, a shared activity
5. Reflect Personally – "What triggered me?"

Arushi's Reflection

I've said "I'm sorry" more as a mother than ever before in life. And strangely, that hasn't weakened my position — it has deepened our bond.

Reflection Prompt

- When was the last time I apologized to my child?
- What did I learn from that moment?

Key Takeaway

Children don't just learn from what we say — but from what we *own*. Say sorry. Show growth.

Chapter 10:

Parenting Partnerships – It Takes Two, and Sometimes More

"When parents unite, children flourish. When families unite, children thrive. "In the journey of parenting, the role of the "village" is often underestimated. The early years of a child's life are built not just on toys and timetables, but on trust, consistency, and cooperation between the key adults around them. Whether it's mom and dad, grandparents, caregivers, or even teachers, the child absorbs the emotional climate around them.

Real-Life Story: Aryan's Two Worlds

Aryan, 4, had recently started throwing tantrums every evening.

His mother felt exhausted. "He doesn't listen to anything I say," she confided. The father, busy with work, believed discipline should be stricter. The grandparents, meanwhile, were indulging Aryan with sweets and screen time. One day, the teacher called them in: "Aryan is confused and emotionally unsettled. At school, he's quiet. At home, he's overwhelmed." That conversation became a turning point. The family sat together and created a unified parenting plan — clear screen limits, consistent responses, and shared responsibilities. Within weeks, Aryan's mood changed. He smiled more. Listened more. Slept better.

Why This Matters

Children need emotional predictability to feel secure. When caregivers contradict each other or pass blame, it creates instability. When they align — even with differing opinions — it builds emotional strength.

What a Strong Parenting Partnership Looks Like

- Consistent Boundaries: Whether it's bedtime or mealtime, consistency builds trust.

- Shared Decision-Making: One parent saying "no" while the other says "yes" confuses a child.

- Regular Communication: Between

spouses, grandparents, or co-parents — keep talking.

•	No Blame Games in Front of Children: Children internalize conflict. Keep adult issues private.

What If You Disagree with Your Partner's Style?

Parenting disagreements are natural. The key is handling them privately and respectfully.

•	Avoid correction in front of children

•	Use "I feel" statements instead of "You never" accusations

•	Make time to align, even if you don't always agree

"Let's talk about this when the kids are asleep. I want us to be on the same page."

☐

Including Grandparents and Extended Family

In Indian households especially, grandparents often play a large role in upbringing. Their wisdom is valuable, but generational gaps can lead to conflict. Balance is the key.

- Involve them in routines
- Respectfully educate them about new-age parenting approaches
- Encourage their bonding time with the child without giving them all control

Arushi's Reflection

There was a time when I felt I was the only one parenting. My husband was supportive, but we weren't always in sync. It showed in our child's reactions. Once we decided to talk, plan, and take turns – it changed everything. Also, as part of a joint family, I had to learn the art of respecting opinions but gently standing my ground. I realized it wasn't about control — it was about collaboration.

☐

Practice Tips

1. Hold Weekly Parenting Check-Ins – no phones, just talk.

2. Divide Roles Respectfully – not all chores are "mom jobs."

3. Build a Family Agreement Chart – even for grandparents!

4.   Praise Each Other's Efforts – children learn appreciation from you.

5.   Don't Undermine Each Other Publicly – present a united front.

Reflection Prompts

- Are we presenting a united front to our child?

- Do we respect each other's parenting contributions?

- Is there someone else (like a grandparent or nanny) who needs to be included in our parenting circle?

Key Takeaway

A strong parenting partnership isn't about perfection. It's about showing up together, learning together, and standing together. When adults unite, children feel safe. And when they feel safe, they soar.

Bonus Chapter: Parenting the Parent – Refilling Your Own Cup

"You are your child's first home. Make sure you are a place of warmth, not weariness."

In every parenting book, workshop, and quote, there's a silent truth often skipped — the parent's heart also needs parenting. While you're nurturing your child's growth, your own strength, sanity, and soul often get left behind. This chapter is not about child-rearing. It's about self-healing. About being the mirror your child learns from, not through perfection, but through inner peace.

Real-Life Reflection: A Silent Cry Behind a Smile

Anjali, a well-respected mother of three, was the go-to mom at every PTA meeting. Always prepared. Always polished. But behind her confident presence, she was battling exhaustion, anxiety, and isolation. One day, while dressing her toddler, she quietly whispered, "I'm tired of being strong."

That was her turning point.

She didn't run away from motherhood — she rebuilt herself within it. She began with 20 minutes of solitude each day. She stopped apologizing for needing space. She reconnected with her hobbies. And for the first time in years, she began smiling not for others — but for herself.

Why Parenting Yourself Changes Everything

A regulated parent raises a safe child.

A joyful parent raises a hopeful child.

A rested parent raises a calm child.

Your emotional state teaches louder than your words.

How to Begin Parenting the Parent

1. Name Your Need

You say "I'm fine" too often.
Pause. Ask yourself: Am I tired?
Overwhelmed? Lonely? Lost?
Naming it helps reclaim it.

2. Heal Your Inner Child

Much of our parenting stress
stems from our own childhood
wounds. Reflect on how you were
parented and gently ask, Am I
repeating patterns or rewriting
them?

3. Stop the Performance

You do not owe anyone a perfect
parent. Let go of curated smiles
and Pinterest-worthy lunchboxes.
Your child needs you, not your
filtered version.

4. Rediscover Joy Beyond Roles

You're not just a mom. Or just a
dad. Or just a teacher.

You are a person. You have
passions. Interests. A heartbeat

that existed before "Mumma" or "Papa" was your name.

5. Create Micro-Moments of Peace

Not everyone can escape for a spa day. But you can take 5 minutes with chai on the balcony. Or 10 minutes to write a journal entry. Or 3 minutes to stand under the sun and breathe.

Gentle Reminders Every Parent Needs

- You're allowed to rest without guilt.

- You're allowed to say "no" even to your child.

- You're allowed to choose yourself, sometimes.

- You're allowed to grow with your child, not just for them.

Arushi's Personal Note

In my own journey, I realized that the days I felt most disconnected from my children were the days I had abandoned myself. Parenting is not about constant sacrifice. It is about sacred balance. You matter. Your healing matters. Your joy matters. Because in giving your child the world, don't lose the wonder within yourself.

Practice Prompts for Gentle Self-Parenting

- What did I do today that made me smile?

- When was the last time I asked myself what I needed?

- • Am I treating myself with the kindness I show my child?

Your Turn: A Loving Challenge

Take a moment. Close your eyes.

Say this aloud (or write it down):

"I am worthy of rest. I am worthy of joy. I am enough. "Now live one moment today from that place of wholeness. Even if it's messy. Even if it's quiet. Even if no one sees it but you.

Parents' Note: Your Journey So Far

Dear Parent,

Before you close this book, take a moment to breathe and reflect on your journey so far. Parenting is rarely easy or linear. It's full of unexpected turns, moments of doubt, overwhelming love, and surprising strength — all mixed into the daily rhythms of life.

Ask yourself:

- What have been your biggest challenges?

- What small victories have you celebrated quietly?

- How have you grown as a parent, as a partner, and as a person?

- What lessons have your children taught you — about patience, joy, or resilience?

There is no perfect way to parent, and there is no finish line. Your best efforts, your presence, and your heart matter more than you know.

Keep cherishing the moments — even the messy, tiring ones — because they are shaping the adults your children will become.

Your journey is unique and valuable. Celebrate it. Learn from it. Keep moving forward with courage and kindness.

Closing Message

One Moment at a Time… Always

Parenting is not about having all the answers — it's about having

the courage to keep learning,
growing, and showing up. There
will be moments of doubt, but
there will also be moments of joy
so deep, it brings tears to your
eyes. If there's one message I
hope stays with you, it is this:

You are doing better than you
think. Every time you choose
connection over control, presence
over perfection, or patience over
punishment — you are raising
them right.

This book is not the end of your
parenting story. It's just a gentle
nudge forward… a reminder to
pause, breathe, and lead your
children with love and intention —
one moment at a time.

With faith in your journey,

– Arushi Mahajan